KENNEDY
AND
HER
COLORFUL
CAPES

WRITTEN BY

KATIE L. BUKOWSKI

This book is dedicated to,

Kyle and Kennedy Bukowski

Thank you to my amazing husband, Kyle, for the love and support, and thank you to my beautiful daughter, Kennedy, for the inspiration to write this book. You remind me every day how important life is and how to find the good in every bad. You are truly a ray of sunshine. Your smile, laugh, and love of life, brightens everyone around.

It's Monday Morning, there's dew on the ground. The birds are chirping such a beautiful sound!

Kennedy wakes out of bed, a big stretch and yawn, and yells with excitement "It's morning it's dawn!"

She runs right to her closet of colorful capes. "Hmm, which one today, what color what shape?

Maybe the green one, it brings out my eyes. No, maybe the black one, I'll be in disguise.

I'll pick purple it's my favorite one. I'll wear it with pride in front of everyone!"

"Kennedy, are you ready." She heard her mother say. "Yes, mom, I'm ready. I am ready for the day!"

Off to school they go, singing out loud.

Kennedy in her cape, and wearing it proud!

Up the sidewalk she goes, skipping along. What a perfect day, nothing could go wrong!

She first sees Miss Violet, then Susie then Jack! They ask, "What are you wearing, what is hanging from your back?"

Kennedy replies, "It's my **amazing** cape, my favorite one! I have so many, more than a ton!"

Susie replies, with almost a frown, "Why a cape and not a crown?"

For just a second Kennedy's heart sinks, she thought, "oh no, did I make a mistake?"

And then she remembers what her mother always says, "Be you, be beautiful, and let your wings spread!"

"I wear a cape to stand out in a crowd. I wear a cape all around! They make me feel special in every way, all the different colors, they brighten my day! I wear a cape like a princess wears her crown, or just like the sheriff who wears his badge around town!"

Her mother just nodded and smiled and gave her a kiss goodbye, and Kennedy walked into school, with her head held high.

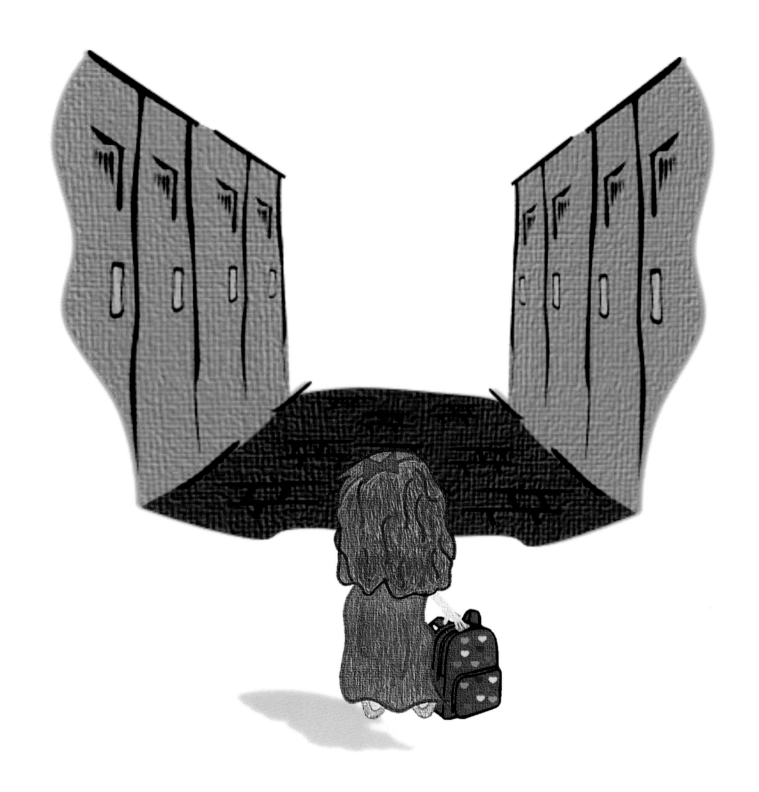

As she went to her locker and put her bag away, right behind her, her purple cape just swayed.

She wore that cape all day long, it made her feel invincible, and mighty, and strong.

As the day went on, and school came to an end,

Kennedy was so excited that she made so many new friends!

The school bell rang and class was dismissed, Kennedy ran to her parents with a hug and a kiss!

She couldn't wait to tell them about her day, where to begin? She had so much to say!

I made some new friends, and one's name is Drew. He LOVED my cape and he wants one in blue!

Penelope and Fred asked for one in RED! They all loved my cape, that's what they said!

Kennedy smiled as she talked about her day. "Which cape tomorrow? I'm thinking pink or gray!"

Then she grabbed her mom's hand and said with glee, "You were right, I should always just be ME!"

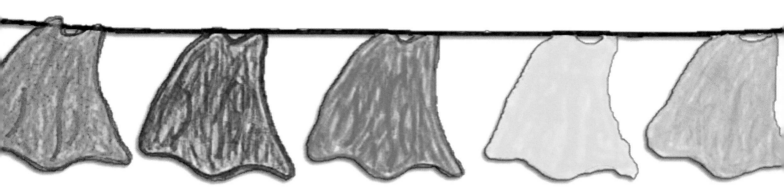

Never be afraid to be who you are!

Never underestimate the power of positivity and love.

It's true what they say,

LOVE conquers all!